Copyright © 2024 by Stephanie Hale

All rights reserved.

BISAC Codes:
POE025000 POETRY / Haiku
POE011000 POETRY / Canadian
POE024000 POETRY / Women Authors

Hardcover ISBN: 978-1-0691039-1-8
Paperback ISBN: 978-1-0691039-0-1
eBook ISBN: 978-1-0691039-2-5

Photograph credit: Alyx, March 2024
Cover photo credit: Rucksack Magazine

First Edition

For Alyx

Thank you for gifting me the idea of this book.

DECADE I

miracle baby

a stargazer from the start

so small in doll clothes

two baby brothers

the best accidents of life

play and fight and love

military brat

found by police in a field

lost searching for dad

innocence of youth
wishing on toilet pennies
plumbers don't come free

oddly auspicious
daddy's little sunshine girl
so much light inside

Alaskan midnights

like Texan summer middays

watch the sun circle

never not growing

language, music, sports, and Scouts

we were busy kids

major concussion

gifted kid gets amnesia

must relearn her past

five syllables here

and seven syllables here

completes a haiku

first real vacation
tenth birthday in Hawaii
submarine surprise

DECADE II

boys on the playground
they'd squish bugs in front of me
laughing when I cried

a black lab puppy

from our neighbour on Christmas

my Penelope

the latest bloomer

last one of my friends to bleed

with gaps in my smile

I've always seen sounds
I thought everyone did
synesthesia

choreography

Tacoma Dance Festival

1920s style

one-time incident

all it takes to change a life

sudden loss of trust

lake of pure turquoise

family backpacking trip

Mount Robson summit

The Adventuress
a 1900s tall ship
sailing Gig Harbor

getting lost in France
after a day at the Louvre
and street harassment

first relationship

ritualistic abuse

learn what love is not

Kochanamachuck

and Chai Latté Death Patrol

save the best for last

six schools in five years
a fridge, the only constant
I grieved when it broke

seventeen years old
a six-year addiction starts
the pain of cutting

the joy of cutting

and painting with my own blood

help – I scare myself

whispered "I love you"s
trading our virginities
seven-year pact broke

Europe trip with mum

Germany, Belgium, and Spain

unforgettable

university

all alone in the real world

far away from home

raped in a dorm room

from classmate to criminal

the school does nothing

second year, new job
a Residence Advisor
no rapes on my watch

working for the school

my boss gives me alcohol

then he sleeps with me

I find small solace

smoking weed to ease the pain

trade up addictions

look with hands and feet

rock-climbing with a blind-fold

difficult ascent

family road trip
I drive us part of the way
goodbye, great grandpa

another winter ends

farewell to my teenage years

not sure I'll miss you

DECADE III

shaved bald on campus
in honour of my grandpa
cancer fundraiser

GNCTR

Technical Report Award

and I got to steer

Research Assistant

x-ray scanning lung samples

the paths of breaths past

representation

woman in engineering

I get called "the boobs"

the world sparkles pink

next, it's my personal Hell

hallucinations

bisexual beau

"better head than a gay man"

that's why he proposed

EDS Type 3

rare genetic disorder

cursed by heritage

twenty-one years old

I am missing thirty pounds

colonoscopy

the results are in

anaphylactic to soy

hunger begets fear

I catch him cheating

he asks for me to join them

my heart is shattered

class with my rapist

I can't take it anymore

medical leave starts

numerology
trying to make sense of life
chaos to cosmos

new psychologist

deep voice sharing deeper words

I call him 'sensei'

the battle begins

seeking justice for my rape

get him off campus

Jamaican sunset

ocean waves and lightning strikes

I propose to him

life is too painful
say goodbye in the mirror
suicide attempt

the battle goes on

a journalist gets involved

I make the front page

pole dancing lessons

a return to confidence

finding my power

a cancelled wedding

boxes packed on Christmas Day

unhappy new year

case chronology

I get drunk every day

this battle sucks balls

pain, pain, go away

come again some other day

or just fuck right off

papier-mâché doll
she's pretty on the outside
but empty inside

remembering Ned

crying in my Cheerios

trying to forget

emaciated

thirty-seven kilograms

eat, sleep, and repeat

Mount Robson, Take 2
remember the turquoise lake
solo adventure

signed, sealed, delivered

watch me lead by example

Human Rights Complaint

a friend visits me

turns out he is a stranger

talk about awkward

last day together
making love in a bookstore
like where we first met

a home library

and coin collection projects

ready for the move

zero, one, zero

just organized entropy

what is a human?

nothing but blue skies

all the world is my oyster

and I am its pearl

consciousness rising

I give a gift to a gift

laughter comes with ease

my volcanic man

make my pyroclastic flow

erupt into me

I long to give you

early morning affections

till late afternoon

polyamory
nihilistic hedonism
I participate

third eye opening

LSD & DMT

I cannot unsee

astral traveling

past life experiences

supernatural

sandpaper kisses

from the one we named after

a season of death

I curl up alone

in the hospital E.R.

and hold my own hand

I keep losing shit
at Paul's place, like my earrings
and my self-respect

twenty-sixth birthday

the day the pandemic starts

cancelled dinner plans

restrictions in place

grandma has her final stroke

lonesome funeral

my return to school

an online music program

jazz violinist

I meet someone new
the feeling of adventure
he moves in with me

BC Supreme Court
I win against my old school
keep moving forward

he wants me baptised

I'm reborn in the ocean

cleansed for our union

wedding in the park

with strangers for witnesses

I'm the princess bride

a circus of suits
arguing about my past
how is this justice?

sacrifice my dreams

abandon second degree

prepare to move east

he spits in my face

and throws me blanket parties

I hate this marriage

I go to the cops
my husband is arrested
separation starts

cab driver rapes me

it was safer to walk home

are all men monsters?

I forget sometimes

we are not in the same boat

just on the same path

bright blue ice cream truck

I sell cones with candy eyes

the children love it

the hearing concludes

return to engineering

start back at square one

we finally meet

after nine months of dating

and lifetimes apart

my first miscarriage

a chemical pregnancy

this small loss is big

a raised garden bed
I plant carrots and flowers
humble first harvest

sentencing hearing

he pleads guilty on all counts

two years probation

the battle is won

exactly six years have passed

we meet that same day

white ribbon speaker
my story in my own words
standing ovation

a new year begins

time to unmask all my pain

I quit smoking weed

my dream job offer

I've waited ten years for this

life just got better

no matter how much

any one person loves me

I love me more first

three-hundred-sixty

a full circle made of months

ends with a first kiss

About the Author

Stephanie Hale is a Civil Engineering Technologist and Human Rights Activist. She resides in British Columbia, Canada. This is her first literary work.

www.ingramcontent.com/pod-product-compliance
Lightning Source LLC
Chambersburg PA
CBHW030452010526
44118CB00011B/898